His Own Simple Gift

by

Helen Clark Hensley

ISBN: 978-1-8381691-5-2

Cover Illustrator: Anna Boles
Editor: Dr. Mary Helen Hensley

All illustrations strictly copyright with the illustrator and author.

www.bookhubpublishing.com
(091) 846953 (087) 2246885
Twitter: @bookhubpublish
Instagram: bookhub_publishing

Book Hub Publishing and the Author are committed to inclusion
and diversity.

Dedication

I dedicate this book, with
gratitude and love, to my
wonderful parents,

Elizabeth Davies Clark and
Dr. Garland Hunt Clark

The year 1951 was a most memorable year for me in so many ways. Graduating in May from Westhampton College of the University of Richmond, in Virginia, started the excitement. Then, being invited to teach English and Journalism at the very high school from which I had graduated just four years earlier, was so special! Winchester High School, in my own hometown of Winchester, Kentucky!

That year really was unforgettable, because at Christmas I became engaged to Dick Hensley, of Martinsville, Virginia, my University of Richmond sweetheart (we had 60 wonderful years together).

Early in those years, Dick gave me a special gift… a beautiful jewelry box with a brass plaque on the top, with my initials inscribed on it.

This book is the result of a discovery in 2020 of yet another thrilling event - that of a hidden gem inside this gift that Dick had given me so many years ago. No, the gem wasn't a diamond or a ruby, it was the original pink, type-written sheets of a Christmas story I had written in 1951. It was hidden for years in a secret pocket inside that unique old jewelry box.

Here's my story! In early December of 1951, I was living at my parents' home while teaching at Winchester High. Each day after classes found me walking from the school to my church, where I worked as Interim Educational Director. Late one afternoon, as I arrived at the front walk of our home, I could see my mother, Elizabeth Davies Clark, waiting at the front door. Mother had an urgent request:

"I need a Christmas story for the December meeting of the Winchester Music Club".

Right after supper, the story was started, and once my pen went to paper, it would not stop. My father, Dr. Garland Clark, arrived home late from his nightly hospital rounds, and asked me what was so *imperative* at that late hour. My answer, "A Christmas story for Mother".

He smiled, nodded and understood. His wife was an extraordinary singer and accomplished pianist, and this club meant the world to her. The story was completed and not only did Mother present it, she lent her angelic voice by singing relative songs such as "I Wonder As I Wander", by fellow Kentuckian, John Jacob Niles.

Soon after, the original pages were tucked away, "out of sight, out of mind". How or when those pink, print-faded type-written pages ended up in the secret pocket of my precious jewelry box remains a mystery.

Luckily, the Christmas story was rediscovered in September, 2020, published, and now, here it is with you. Never did I dream this would be the final destination… in *your* hands! I feel honored and humbled and my wish is that this is a gift that keeps on giving for years to come. Pass it on!

Finding this hidden 'Christmas Gem', nearly 70 years later, made 2020, a highlight of my 91st year. After re-reading the story all these years later, it was evident that its message is timeless and priceless, for the

best gifts of all are the simple ones from
the heart.

My heartfelt thanks to Book Hub Publishing
in County Galway, Ireland, and to Athlone,
Ireland's, Anna Boles, who has gifted us all
with her wonderfully inspired illustrations.
They are magical!

May "His Own Simple Gift" become your own
Christmas Gem.

In the Spirit of Christmas,

Helen Clark Hensley

The Spirit of Christmas

The story that I'm going to
tell

Takes place in a town you know
quite well.

So, to be in keeping with
social graces,

I won't unmask these fictional
faces.

The Spirit of Christmas
saturated the air,

And like a great epidemic was
caught everywhere.

A Santa Claus chuckled in every
large store,

And King Christmas reigned as
never before.

The Holly Man called, "Merry
Christmas", to hear it,

And shops featured books on
True Christmas Spirit.

The street was crowded with a
gift searching throng,

Who like Wassailers of old,
moved gaily along.

An empty-handed boy was soon
caught in the current

Of the swift moving stream, but
he knew what it meant.

He knew it was Christmas, the
Holly Man said so,

But why the commotion, he still
didn't know.

He studied the faces and
wondered if they

Know just why they were
breathless
And rushing that way.

He looked into their arms with
presents so full,

Then at his empty hands, and
again felt a pull

At his heart and his coat, as
he stepped in the way

Of a man with a tree, who had
only one day

To prepare for the Yuletide
celebration,

And provide for *his children* a
day of elation.

No present had the boy to give
Christmas morn,

And he looked at his own
clothes, ragged and worn,

And wished for others less
fortunate than he,

Something could be offered that
they might see

The Spirit of Giving was first
in his mind,

'Tho no gift had he, of any
kind.

His Own Simple Gift

As the child trudged homeward
the force became lighter,

To compensate for the darkness
the stars twinkled brighter.

He had far to walk and much
time to think

Of the gifts to be given, and
then he would sink

To the depths of despair his
young mind could grasp,

For not one gift to give did
his hands enclasp.

His Own Simple Gift

The houses got smaller, the
street was now narrow,

But the thoughts of the child
were all for the 'morrow

When mankind would give gifts
both large and small,

And a sad voice cried out,
"I have nothing at all."

His Own Simple Gift

And the same little voice lent
its sorrow to song,

Its appeal touched the night as
he walked slowly on.

And the stars in their pity
blinked tears from their eyes,

To see a giftless boy throwing
his lament to the skies.

As the boy caught sight of the
shack he called home,

He knew it was useless to
wander and roam

In search of a gift one could
feel and could see,

When his could be heard...
"It's here! It's in me!"

New hope was born in him, he
shouted for joy

And changed his direction to
present his new 'toy'…

"I'll give them my song…
before it's too late.

I will get to give, and 'tho
it's not great

I'll sing to all I can get to
tonight.

I'll make someone happy…
my present's just right!"

He had no time to waste as he
ran through the streets,

'Til at last he appeared at the
houses where treats

Were a usual thing...
so, he skipped up the walk

And knocked at the door, could
hear laughter and talk

From within, and he knew
that his gift was for all,

And not just the few.

An annoyed lady opened the door

just a crack

And on seeing the lad cried,

"Alas and Alack!

Can't you see that we're busy

and don't want to buy

Of your peddler's ware. Oh, how

I do try

To keep calm and serene under
these circumstances,

When my time is so filled with
parties and dances."

"But lady, I don't want to sell
you a thing...

Just want to wish you well by
tryin' to sing."

But the lady was gone and the
boy shook his head

And wondered why he, to this
house, had been led.

But he MUST give his present,
so he ran quickly down

To the next block of houses,
nearer the town.

He rang a great bell and waited
to see

What type of person his
recipient would be.

A man appeared this time, and
the child sang with glee,

Until, "On your way urchin,
we're trimming our tree.

We've no food to give you, so
run on along."

And the child knew that
hopeless, was the gift of his
song.

His Own Simple Gift

He turned again homeward,
though blinded by tears,

"Don't they know why we've
celebrated for all of these
years?

Don't they know why the
presents are in all their
places?

Don't they know that it's
Christmas for ALL of the races?

They've forgotten the sweet
little Jesus boy

Made Christmas for me, too,
so I can spread joy."

And he flung himself down, then
looked up above,

And singing through tears, gave
a gift wrapped in love

To the One who would listen and
never reject

The most humble of gifts He
could ever expect.

The boy's eyes were wide as he
sang of the Child,

And pictured His face...
compassionate and mild.

When suddenly he sensed a light
so strong

That he covered his face and
ended his song.

Through tiny fingers he saw to
his fright,

A boy just his size, dressed
all in white.

And 'round him was shining such
a radiant glow,

That the trembling boy
whispered,
"I know; I know.

You're my little Jesus boy,
Oh! Say that it's so!"

But the child in white said,
"Just an angel am I...

Can't you tell by my harp?" And
then with a sigh,

"I came down to thank you for
your priceless gift.

Why, it even gave us angels a
lift."

Tears of gratitude welled in
the small boy's eyes

And he sobbed, looking up in
wonder and surprise.

"But why are you so kind, I'm
not like you, you see?

You're shiny and bright, yet
you care about me?"

The angel put his arms around
his new little friend

And explained how he happened
to earth to descend.

"Why, we all heard your music
and its sound we adore,

It was pure and unselfish and
perfect and more.

It was ALL that you had and you
gave it away.

Angels will be humming it for
many a day.

But it's a shame your music's
ignored here on earth,

Where folks need to remember
the day of *His* birth.

So, I've come to help you
spread joy among mortals,

For this reason I left my
heavenly portals.

Now, this is my plan...
I hope you'll agree.

Tomorrow is Christmas Day and
so we can..."

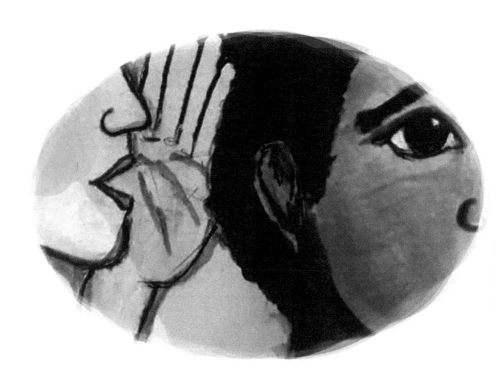

And the little angel whispered
in his kindred friend's ear,

And a visible light of joy did
appear

On the face of the one who
thought all was in vain,

For now he was cleansed of
every tear stain.

His face was shining, for to
ALL he could give

His own simple gift, for which
he would live.

Daylight was breaking as they
completed their plan,

And into the sunlight they
walked, hand in hand.

'Til the grateful boy stopped
and wrinkled his nose...

"I can't walk with an angel,
just look at these clothes!

They're ragged and dirty,
you're spotless and clean.

You go on ahead...
I mustn't be seen."

"Don't worry," said the angel,
"I know what we'll do.

We'll exchange clothes, then
we'll both feel brand new."

So the fair little angel donned
rags, dirty and tight,

While his new friend was a
contrast of color and light.

One's face was angelic, and the
clothes were black,

But even in rags, no beauty did
lack.

The other face colorful, in a
robe spotless white.

Both faces and hearts shed a
radiant light.

They made a strange sight on
that new Christmas day,

Walking together, carefree and
gay,

So that all who saw them felt
sure they were dreaming,

And stood rubbing their eyes,

while the two went by scheming.

The great Christmas service was
now at hand,

Crowds rushed to the cathedral
like a mighty band

Of pilgrims reaching their
destination,

Waiting for a special Christmas
sensation.

His Own Simple Gift

In the church sat the shoppers
who were yesterday

Too busy to notice a boy in
their way.

Through the door came the
'lady' to take her place,

Who thought a poor boy a social
disgrace.

On the first row sat the Elder
for all to see,

He had no time for an 'urchin',
while trimming his tree.

The carols were sung, the
scripture was read,

And the choir in the
"Hallelujah Chorus" was led.

As the very last strain of the
anthem was heard,

A most unusual thing occurred;

Helen Clark Hensley

From apparently nowhere a clear
voice chimed out,

Unseen by all, yet audibly
devout.

And the story it told bore a
message sharp:

One Voice accompanied by an
angel's harp.

The notes resounded from every
eve,

All were held spellbound and
could not leave,

Nor were they capable of
expressing their joy

At the song of a hidden,
invisible boy.

For behind the great pipes of
the organ they play,

Had waited two little boys
since the break of day.

Both were unseen, as ALL great
things are,

But their music was heard by
folks near and far...

For they sang out the message
which years cannot tire,

And both were accompanied by an
angelic choir.

The music was ended, all fell
to their knees,

And thoughts just of others
dominated their pleas.

A new people left the church
that morn,

A new meaning of Christmas,

had in each, been reborn.

The church was deserted, except
for the two,

Who walked down the aisle and
secretly knew

That theirs was a gift long
awaited by man,

And down to the front steps the
two quickly ran.

The dear little boy looked
longingly up,

And pointed to Heaven with a
motion abrupt.

He asked from the heart, "Can I
come, too?"

The angel replied, "No, I'll
come to you."

So, now on Christmas in lands
far and wide,

Imagine two figures, side by
side, and

If you hear hidden music when
the church choir is through,

In angelic harmony, clear and
true,

You'll know it's two boys who
meet every year,

An angel from Heaven and his
best friend from here.

They sing of a world full of
colorful faces,

Of kindness and caring for ALL
of the races.

It's their gift to you, with a
meaning sharp...

*ONE VOICE accompanied by an
angel's harp.*

Illustrations by Anna Boles

Anna Boles lives in Athlone, Ireland, where she creates wonderful art. She loves to paint and Ireland provides her with many beautiful scenes, which she likes to transfer to canvas in her own unique style.

Anna loves to express herself in her paintings through color and she loved creating the illustrations for this book.

You can view and purchase Anna's work online via many social media websites as well as on her own website at www.annmarieboles.

Facebook: @annasartpage
Twitter: @AnnaBoles3
Instagram: @anna.boles

Helen at the Quiet Man Bridge in Connemara
County Galway, Ireland, in 2018

CPSIA information can be obtained
at www.ICGtesting.com
Printed in the USA
BVHW022247081220
595180BV00009B/208

9 781838 169152